LONDON in the NINETIES

LONDON in the NINETIES

Edited by
Leonora Collins

Republished EP Publishing Limited, 1972
First published The Saturn Press, London, 1950

Republished 1972 by EP Publishing Limited
East Ardsley, Wakefield
Yorkshire, England

by kind permission of the
copyright holder

ISBN 0 85409 905 0

Please address all enquiries to EP Publishing
Ltd.
(address as above)

Reprinted in Great Britain by
Scolar Press Limited, Menston, Yorkshire

London in the Nineties

Edited by Leonora Collins

LONDON

in the

NINETIES

SATURN PRESS

FIRST PUBLISHED IN 1950 BY The Saturn Press

28 Southampton Street, London, W.C.2

PRINTED BY The Vandyck Printers Limited

London and Bristol

THE BOOK DESIGNED BY Ronald Ingles, M.S.I.A.

LONDON, in the eighteen-nineties. . . . We always hear them called the " naughty " nineties, but what were they really like ? What did people do ? What did they look like ? How did they earn a living—travel—amuse themselves ? Where did they live, and in what sort of houses ? What did they talk about ? Was the life of the average Londoner of fifty years ago, and his tastes and background, as different from that of his present-day counterpart as the Imperialism of Joseph Chamberlain is from the modern conception of Commonwealth ?

By 1890, many of the burning ethical battles of the century were over. Darwin, Newman and Bradlaugh were passing into history. Women had already gained so much social and legal independence that some commentators thought their freedom unseemly and even dangerous. The stage, the arts and literature were less stifled by the excessive prudery and overwhelming impulse to preach which had been prevalent for almost the whole of the Victorian era. That era covered the conscious lifetime of most of the Queen's subjects.

Twenty years of free education and forty of unparalleled commercial prosperity had helped to produce a working and middle class eager for information and entertainment. Conditions of work, too, were gradually becoming better. While some East End factories and workshops were still sordid and filthy, with wages at a minimum and hours practically unregulated, many firms were finding the advantages of organisation and cleanliness over haphazard " sweating," and the trade unions were becoming extremely strong and responsible bodies.

Conditions in the City itself were slowly altering its appearance. The old chop-houses were giving way to something more like the cafés of to-day, eating-places which put convenience before former customs. Traffic, although it was still thick and confused, moving at the pace of the lumbering drays with their great horses, was nevertheless somewhat eased by the Underground, which was now widely used. Although formality in dress was still an unassailable rule, there was less difference than ever before between the appearance of the Director and that of his clerk. Hours were shorter and offices more comfortable, and the lady " typewriter " was starting to make her appearance.

The Londoner's home, if it had any pretension to be up-to-date, was no longer draped in heavy, dark-coloured materials. It was more likely to be very full of fans, peacock's feathers, and curious " novelties "—small objects which were sometimes designed to be useful, and always disguised as something quite different. Wallpaper nearly always had a repetitive pattern ; shawls and china were very popular.

Entertaining of guests, among all classes, was still largely a domestic matter. Ladies were only very gradually venturing to go to restaurants, but luxury fruit, confectionery and groceries of all kinds were increasingly easy to get. The diet of everyone except the very poor was becoming more varied, if not more nutritious, as tinned foods grew safer and so more popular among all classes.

The main outside amusement of the Londoner, whatever his income, opinions or education, was the theatre, from the cheap, old-fashioned melodrama to the Lyceum productions of Shakespeare, and from the rich vulgarity of the music-hall to the much-debated new plays about topical social questions. Every suburb, one might almost say every slum, had a theatre of some sort within easy distance, and in the West End of London the music-hall, the drama, musical-comedy, burlesque, modern comedy, the opera and all the other aspects of the theatre flourished. Open-air entertainment could be found at Earl's Court and the Crystal Palace, or at the Zoo.

There were signs that the barriers between social groups were becoming less rigid ; business-men, foreigners and professional men entered and married into Society, and brides from the United States and the theatre were teaching it to amuse itself in new, more sophisticated ways. Nevertheless, Mayfair still led a very carefully regulated life as a community. At certain times of the year the houses of the aristocracy and of the very rich filled for the Season, and at certain times of the day carriages paraded in the

Park. Children went out with nurses or governess, all the little girls of one family dressed alike. There would be parties, receptions, balls, " drums " and dinners. The shops of Oxford Street, Regent Street and Bond Street showed their " collections." The Opera audience, in full dress, was brilliant, and sometimes bored, but it was the most fashionable entertainment. When the Season ended, the dresses and uniforms, the liveried footmen and starched nursemaids, the window boxes and stiff little park chairs would vanish, leaving the squares of Belgravia and St. James's and the streets of Mayfair almost deserted.

In spite of enormous improvements since the dark days of the middle of the century, there was still a great gulf between the conditions of life of the rest of the community and that of the very poor Londoner. In east London, particularly, there were miles of monotonous streets—not slums, but tall brown tenements and small, cramped houses, relieved only by dark little shops and garish, rather incongruous public houses. Here, in these streets, lived people who were not very interested for the most part in the world outside their own district. Their work was usually hard and often monotonous, their diversions limited to the public-house, an occasional visit to a local music-hall and a jaunt as far as Hampstead Heath on Bank Holiday. Drinking, fighting and swearing were common among men and women. Very few visitors came to these areas from outside, except for the members of the various church missions and the ladies whose activities varied from useful and sensible social work to intermittent " slumming " stunts.

Religious and lay social workers were more concerned with the true slums—a term which covered large districts which had suffered poverty, municipal neglect and social degeneration for varying periods of time and were only just beginning to attract the shocked attention of the more fortunate outside world. Even more wretched were the " submerged " Londoners, men and women who had not got a permanent home in the most verminous and overcrowded hovel, but who generally preferred the hazards of a vagrant life to the certain hardships and humiliations of the casual wards.

Certain areas of East London were rapidly becoming to be almost entirely inhabited by foreign immigrants, a large proportion of whom were refugees from the Russian pogroms. By industry, thrift and driving ambition towards better educational

7

and material standards, many of these people escaped from their overcrowded rooms and " sweat-shops," but at first maintained their individuality and some self-respect by holding to the clothes, customs and languages of their birthplace. The Chinese already had their own quarter in Limehouse, but the Japanese were more likely to be found in Bloomsbury, studying English, and particularly English business customs and methods.

The numerous facets of London's life were not brought under one governing body until 1888, when the London County Council was constituted. The suburbs, the foreign quarters, even the slums, now became as much a part of the official capital as Mayfair or the Strand. The whole vast area of London had become an entity, and writers and artists of all kinds, as well as politicians and business-men, began to see that all the people who lived there must be included in any conception of " Londoners."

To cater for a public which ranged from barely literate to highly academic in education, and from ribald to precious in outlook, a large number of magazines were started at this time, while the established periodicals had for several years been gaining new readers. A policy of quick descriptive reporting of events of general concern followed the very successful example of the young popular newspapers, and articles were also filled with easily assimilated facts and gossip about well-known people. While not so ephemeral in interest as the daily press, these magazines reflect the manners and interests of the world in which they were published.

The first news photograph was printed in a London paper in 1890, and technical and artistic developments in photography made this the first period which we can see naturally through the lens of the contemporary camera, without the poses and conventions of earlier days. Some subjects were still left to the wood-engravers and other illustrators, but in general they were being ousted by the quicker and more realistic medium.

Since it is the aim of this book to give some picture of the ordinary life of a place and period, we have gone almost entirely to the photographer and the periodical journalist for material. It is they, between them, who give a fair contemporary picture, neither too optimistic nor too gloomy, perhaps rather superficial, but certainly not misleading, of life in the London Nineties.

Queen Victoria's Diamond Jubilee service on the steps of St. Paul's

Surely, in some dark corner of every camera, there lurks a good fairy who enchants every plate as it is exposed. The enchantment may not be, is not, obvious at first—it does not make the developed plate less hideous, less harshly mechanical. Yet the enchantment is there, nevertheless, and, after the lapse of years, it fills the photograph with a curious grace. The very coarseness and crudity of the process are turned to good use. In very virtue of its unintelligent realism, an old photograph gains a pathos which is to be found in old pictures.

" A GROUP OF MYRMIDONS " by MAX BEERBOHM.

9

10

Cheapside and
the Mansion House

Holborn Viaduct

Fleet Street, 1900

11

Ludgate Hill from Ludgate Circus, 1900

So far as I can, I avoid that channel of all that is unloveliest in London, the Strand. Some folk profess a charm in it. Me it has repelled always. Was ever anywhere so monotonous a current of harsh faces as flows there? Anxiety, poverty and bedragglement on the pavement, and drivers cursing one another in the blocked traffic; hoarse hucksters on the curb, and debauchees lolling before the drinking bars—the charm of the scene is rather too abstruse for me, I admit.

" PRETENDING " by MAX BEERBOHM.

13

Cockspur Street, St. James's

Near Waterloo Bridge

Morleys Hotel, Charing Cross

15

" We believe that in the future, as in the past, the proportionate numbers of the destitute will gradually diminish, and that individual sinners will be rescued through the agency of religion and of sympathetic friendship ; but as long as vice and drunkenness exist, suffering will follow in their train. Much has been done and is being done, both by public and private effort, to attack the evils at their source. The results of such efforts are slow and gradual, but they are sure. Meanwhile we must not forget the existence of the Poor Law. While it is in force no person can, except of his own free-will, either starve or pass the night in the open air."

H. CLARENCE BOURNE, reviewing
William Booth's " IN DARKEST ENGLAND."
Murrays Magazine Vol. ix. 1891.

Mansion House, 1898

London has never been better supplied with an omnibus service. There are two great companies together with a number of private vehicles. The trams carry a great many persons also, but as a rule they are useful to the clerks rather than to the city men. There are also cabs for those who can afford them. The underground railway carries its tens of thousands. How are these persons distributed ? There are immense cities standing in a belt round London called suburbs. The quarters known as Dalston, Brixton, New Cross, Forest Hill, Walthamstow, Tottenham which accommodate an immense number of clerks. Kennington, Stockwell, Camberwell, contain a large number of City tradesmen. Such suburbs as Balham, Sydenham, Highgate, Hampstead, Barnes, Richmond and others contain the richer sort.

LONDON IN THE NINETEENTH CENTURY by SIR WALTER BESANT.

Horse bus, knife board type, 1891

The policeman controls the slum of 1898 ; ladies visit it ; the clergy know all the people ; one is neither murdered nor robbed ; the worst that can happen is to be mistaken for a School Board official, when things may be poured upon your head and broken plates may fly across the street and knock off your hat.   There is great improvement in cleanliness ; there is more water ; the worst of the old courts have been swept away or rebuilt ; the paving is whole ; a gas lamp burns in it all night ; the sanitary arrangements are more decent.   Overcrowding, drunkenness, dirt, depravity, there is still in plenty, but in every one of these respects there is improvement.

LONDON IN THE NINETEENTH CENTURY

Slum recreation in the London streets, 1903

The dinner hour : roadmenders in New Bridge Street

The Muffin Man (opposite) and the knife cleaner

Match-seller, Ludgate Hill

24

The Paper Boy

25

The last of the Horse-drawn Trams

26

It was a magnificent moment. The very pick of English chivalry stood ready to make the charge. The intervening space between them and the object of the attack was filled with cavalry. The horses dashed past with the sound of thunder . . .

And what was the incident ? Was it a battle ? Was it a siege ?

No ; the incident was something far more interesting.

A man had passed a London crossing, and, marvellous to relate, had not been killed.

No ; nor even wounded.

"PUNCH." 16.4.1898.

The Watercart

On Sunday nights there is, thanks to the County Council's idea of the Day of Rest, no music at Frascati's, the nearest approach London has to a café. Yet only last Sunday afternoon no less than six discordant bands brayed past my study window, some on their way, I presume, to a demonstration in Hyde Park, others to advertise the Salvation Army. It is bad enough that London on the Sabbath should be transformed into a wilderness. That it should be a howling winderness is still worse.

" PICK-ME-UP." 11.5.95.

The Salvation Army, "Hallelujah lads and lasses"
passing down Whitechapel Road, Stepney

Sunday Bathing in the Serpentine

On the Embankment

Opposite : Covent Garden

Covent Garden Market

The market, with its motley display of buyers and sellers, is an animated and picturesque sight. The display of vegetables is wondrous. The piled and well-packed waggons and carts begin to arrive about midnight, are marshalled in the streets leading to the market, and begin to dispose of their loads about four in the morning. The vegetables and fruit are sold in the open space in the centre, flowers in the new flower market which extends into Wellington Street. When the wholesalers and larger dealers have made their purchases, and trade is slackening, the stock remaining is disposed of, chiefly to costermongers, by a sort of Dutch auction. To see the supply of fruit and vegetables carted off, 7 a.m. is early enough. To enjoy the sight and smell of flowers and fruit, the finest in the world, any time from 10 a.m. to 4 or 5 p.m. will answer. The centre arcade at midday is a pretty sight, but not what it once was. Saturday is the best day.

"LONDON PAST AND PRESENT" by HENRY B. WHEATLEY. 1891.

Caledonian Market

32

Victoria Park

Holborn : a children's concert with the Mayor

Playtime in a London School

Above : L.C.C. Snowfield School, Bermondsey, 1894

Below : Orange Street School, 1894

. . . One by one the patients were called up with a " Now then, Mum! " " Let's have a look at that kid of yours, Missus! " " Bring that squint here! " " Come along, Redhead! " " Here you are, Dust-oh! " Little ripples of amusement began to run through the room, many pairs of eyes turning to me for sympathy, and saying as plainly as eyes could do : " Lord bless him, ain't he a funny gentleman ? " It was observable, too, that nobody took offence at his free-and-easy method of address. Even " Redhead," who wore the garb of a hospital nurse, and was much above the rest in social station, only laughed and shrugged her shoulders a little deprecatingly. . . . As for the babies, they came up close to him as confidingly as if they had known him all their lives, and seldom failed to respond at once when, trying to get a good look at their poor little weak eyes, he chirruped at them and said " Now, then, Minnie "—or Gracie, or Johnny —he was never at a loss for a name . . . I suppose the average time given to each was about three minutes, more to a new patient, less to some of the old ones. . . .

" A VISIT TO A LONDON EYE-HOSPITAL " : All the Year Round, vol. ix. 1893.

In Lambeth Palace Grounds—"Archbishop's Park"

40

Hampstead Heath

At the Zoological Gardens,

An Actress of 1900

She was a magnificent woman—there is no other word to express her—who admitted to twenty-five. As a matter of fact, I knew she was at least ten years older, though she never looked it. Her photographs, in tights for the most part, were in all the shop windows of London.

"PICK-ME-UP." 4.5.95.

. . . This is one of the roughest houses in a very rough neighbourhood, but no fault can be found with the management. At the present moment the customers are equally quiet. They number about fifty and are scattered along the bar in the different compartments, some sitting down, more standing up, smoking and talking quietly. Itinerant vendors of matches and penny songs come and go . . . What are they drinking? At the superior end some Scotch whiskies may be seen, a young sailor orders a rum hot, and a woman of the pavement at my elbow asks for a two of gin cold; . . . but for the rest it is all beer. Several kinds of beer are sold at these houses, but the working-man confines himself mainly to the two cheapest, which are technically called " beer " and " ale." The former is a very dark opaque liquid of the same colour as porter, but much weaker, and it costs 3d. the pot (i.e. quart) or 1d. the glass. " Ale " otherwise called " Four-ale " or " Mild," is clear but rather dark in colour, and costs 4d. the pot or 1d. the glass . . .

. . . Two workmen come in perfectly sober, and one of them stands treat for two glasses of ale. His mate is in the act of drinking when the door opens, and two terrible-looking women rush in. The older is a wretched hag, who has already " had a drop," the other, a big, heavily-built woman, is perfectly sober and in deadly, tragic earnest . . .

" So I've caught you, have I, ye scoundrel? Drinking again? And where did you get the money from?" she shrieks.

" This gentleman gave me a glass of beer, that's all," sheepishly answers the man, indicating his friend.

" Then he's as bad as you, ye scoundrel. You've left me and the children to starve —me and the four bits of children. Ay," she continued, raising her voice and shouting at him for everyone to hear, " you had two pounds on Friday, and what did you bring home for me and the children? Not one farthing—not that much! You took it all, and us with nothing in the house. And when you come home drunk and I rummaged in your pockets, like a thief, what did I find? Seven and threepence. Two pounds on Friday night and spent it all but seven and threepence among the—ye—scoundrel! "

She drags him to the door, thrusts him through, and as he disappears bangs him savagely between the shoulders. . . .

. . . I lately saw a respectable-looking couple take four young children into a public-house, and when they came out they were all wiping their mouths. . . . It is done, I believe, out of ignorance and thoughtlessness from a mistaken idea of kindness. The affection of parents of that class takes the form of giving their children whatever they have themselves. . . .

"THE ENGLISH PUBLIC-HOUSE" by ARTHUR SHADWELL. The National Review. 1895.

Late Victorian Interior

It may be questioned . . . whether the decorative treatment of the walls should give place to pictures in rooms which are occupied from day to day. If we imagine the tired man of business returning to his suburban home in the evening, it can hardly be supposed that he will be in a position to make the special mental effort involved in inspecting his pictures; but supposing him to be the happy possessor of a harmoniously decorated room, he will be at once soothed and charmed by its very atmosphere. It will not be necessary for him to study the pattern of the wall-paper or the carpet to feel the influence imparted by the ordered beauty of his surroundings. It is in the air like music, and a man may leave such a room without being able to render an intelligible account of anything in it, and yet have felt its charm to the full.

"THE DECORATION OF THE SUBURBAN HOME" by H. BAILLIE SCOTT. Studio 1895.

A dining room in an English Home

Bedroom designed and furnished in 1900

50

Forder Bros. and Co., 121, Long-acre

Original Inventors of the FORDER HANSOM

No connexion with any other firm of the same name.

Forder's Hansoms have been supplied to

Her Majesty the Queen,

His Royal Highness the Prince of Wales,

Princes, noblemen and gentlemen throughout the world.

Forder Bros. respectfully invite all American visitors to view, at 121, Long-acre, some new Hansoms, and part of a large order for the London Railway, New York.

Advertisement in The Times. 1893.

Hansom Cab, 1898

The City and South London Railway, 1890

Third Class Dining Car on the Great Northern Railway

A West End Photographer's Studio and (opposite) a flashlight portrait

On the steps of St. Paul's Cathedral : July 6th, 1893,
watching the wedding procession of Princess Mary and the Duke of York

56

The Duke and Duchess of York (later King George V and Queen Mary) after the marriage

A Sunday evening with the family

We insist on chaperoning our girls, not because we do not trust them, as I have heard some folks sneeringly insinuate ; nor because we do not trust our friends as some young women have angrily put it ; but because we wish to keep the women-children as long as we may " unspotted from the world." . . . Is a girl improved in any way by having to fight for her own hand, to defend herself from the man she does not care for, from the wiles of the rival she has to look out for ? Is it not better for her, and for the husband who may come, that we should do the fighting and the looking-out for her ? That we

58

should find the man, and then leave her with her powers unimpaired and her eyes clear, with the clearsightedness that only light-heartedness can give, to make up her mind and enable him to make up his mind, concerning the future for them both? . . .

" IN DEFENCE OF WORLDLY MOTHERS " by THE COUNTESS OF DESART.

The National Review, Vol 29. 1897.

A Sunday group, 1897

60

Boating at Richmond, 1892

River Festival at Henley-on-Thames

The Tower Bridge, completed in 1894

When blue-flies tease the slumbr'ous brow
   And water-carts are busy,
When London's dusty pavements glow
   Enough to make one dizzy.
'Tis time to quit the bustling Strand,
   And scent the fields of clover,
And dream away in Lotus-land,
   Till summer days are over.
A boat afloat, a cloudless sky,
   A nook that's green and shady,
A cooling drink, a pigeon-pie,
   A lobster, and a lady !

Anon.   1895.

" PICK-ME-UP."

The Picnic Party

Cycling day in Rotten Row, 1895

66

I wish that Fashion's neglect could doom the bicycle. Of course, it cannot. The bicycle, long before it became fashion's foible, had all the makings of a national institution, and Fashion's patronage has but speeded its triumphal progress through England. Some things were created by Fashion herself, and perished so soon as she was weary of them. Others, merely adopted by her, are more abiding. Golf, for example, as the most perfect example of national stupidity, has an assured, unchequered future, and croquet, as the one outdoor game at which people can cheat, will never be in prolonged abeyance, and bicycling, as a symptom of that locomotomania produced by usage of steam, will endure " till we go back to the old coaches." The bicycle is complementary to the steam engine, doing for the horseless individual what the steam-engine does for the community. It was as inevitable as it is unlovely, and I must put up with it. For the proletariat, it is not merely a necessity, but a great luxury, too. It gratifies that instinct which is common to all stupid people, the instinct to potter with machinery. In the hours of his leisure, if he be not riding, the cyclist is oiling his machine, or cleaning it when it is quite clean, or letting the air out of it for the simple pleasure of inflating it, or unscrewing it, or turning it upside down, or tapping it suspiciously with a pair of pincers. The sight of him is instructive. A mother's solicitude is not more tender than his. Observe him!

" FASHION AND HER BICYCLE " by MAX BEERBOHM. 1899.

The correct hour for riding in the Park is said to be rather earlier this year than last. This only means, I imagine, that Society is to have a longer day, not that its movements are to be any less rapid than usual. Next year's Divorce Court chronicles will, I have no doubt, prove to us that during the season of 1895 Society lived fully up to its reputation.

"PICK-ME-UP." 25.5.95.

OLD LADY : Yes, my dear, it is very interesting. I remember, when I was a girl, going
to see the first train pass through Bath, just as you went to see these motor-cars.

SMALL BOY : Hallo, TOMMY ! My guvnor's given me ten bob, and SMITH minor
and me are going to make a motor-car, &c., &c.

OLD GENTLEMAN : I think I'll take some shares, the papers are full of it. My belief is
the motor-cars, &c., &c.

YOUNG LADY : It would have been rippin' if the weather hadn't been so awful. I biked
as far as Croydon. I'm awfully keen now on ridin' in a motor-car, &c., &c.

INFANT (in a legal sense) : I say, you fellows, private hansoms ain't in it. I've just
ordered a motor. Take TOTTIE de VERE down to Brighton. Rippin' lark.

70

Never told the beastly counter-jumper how old I was. And he can't get anything out of the guvnor. Some old bally judge said fizz is a " necessary," but motor-cars, &c., &c.

INFANT (in every sense) : Boo-hoo! Don't like dolly. Don't like Nana. Naughty Nana. Me want dada give me a moo-car, &c., &c.

CABMAN : What I arsts is, wot am I a-goin' ter do with my bloomin' hoss. If these 'ere motor-cars, &c., &c.

DOCTOR : How about JONES and his pair now? Awful sell for him! Wonder how soon I can leave off jobbing some old screw, and start a motor-car, &c., &c.

UNDERTAKER : A henterprisin' firm must move with the times. Must see about hadvertisin' my " Gothic Glass-panelled Necropolitan Motor-Car, registered." That'll fetch 'em. " Gothic " halways does, and now these motor-cars, &c., &c.

" PUNCH." 28.11.96.

Daimler Dog-cart, 1896

. . . Four steamers were on the spot in eight minutes. After this, steamers followed in quick succession, and in thirty minutes 19 steamers were on the scene, with a complement of long ladders and escapes. Steamers and other appliances continued to arrive until the total number reached fifty-one, one manual engine, one hosecart, three long ladders, two fire-escapes, and three hose and coal-vans. The force consisted of the chief officer, the second officer, three superintendents, and two hundred and eighty-eight officers and men. . . . The astonishing rapidity of the fire was entirely due to the nature of the buildings, the stock which they contained, the distribution of enclosed courts and well-holes, numerous communications in party walls, and the narrowness and relative position of the thoroughfares. It is of interest to note that the quantity of water drawn from the mains of the New River Company for the purpose of extinguishment was 15,000,000 gallons . . . All the water required was drawn from the mains of the Company, who, it may be added, will receive no payment in respect thereof.

" THE GREAT FIRE IN CRIPPLEGATE " : CITY PRESS, 19.11.97.

(Victoria and Albert Museum Library.)

London Firemen

The uniform has very little to do with a soldier's popularity with the ladies, in my opinion. Take, for instance, the headdress. " Tommy " does not walk about the town with his busby on. . . . Soldiers, especially British soldiers, ALWAYS go in to win ; it is that which makes them so confident with the ladies. They do not flaunt their " fair prospects " in the face of their " best girl." She knows that the remuneration of the soldier is scarcely sufficient to keep himself. This fact either furnishes him with an impetus to succeed in his profession, or the girl declares that she is willing to wait until his time has expired.

Girls of the present day do not require a sickly, insipid being for a husband, therefore they prefer the soldier, who is healthy, well-set, and often good-looking.

From a contribution by " DRAGOON." Answers, 30.5.91.

Basket Carrier Tricycle

Recruiting Sergeants at Westminster
waiting outside a Public House for likely recipients of the "Queen's Shilling"

The Jews' Market, Wentworth Street, in the East End, on the day
of the Passover feast

St. Giles's Market, Seven Dials

78

The Strand
from the Golden Cross Hotel

In London Streets : the Bank (opposite) and St. James's

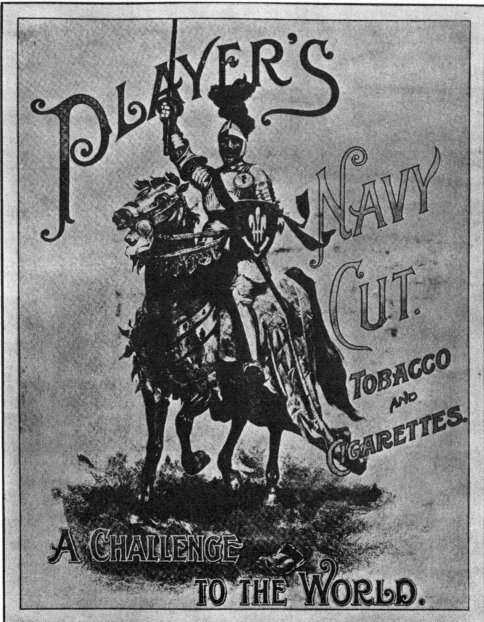

A CHALLENGE TO THE WORLD.

Player's Navy Cut Tobacco

is sold only in 1oz. Packets, 2, 4, 8, and 16oz. Tins.   Mild in Red Packets
and Tins, Medium in Blue Packets and Tins.

Player's Navy Cut Cigarettes

in Packets containing 6 and 12, and Tins of 24, 50, and 100.

The idea of taxing advertisements is an absurd one, because the tax would eventually come out of the pockets of the public and would not limit the prevalence of posters. Besides, the majority of people do not want to limit them. Those who can recall the drab hoarding that for weeks surrounded the plot of ground at the back of the National Gallery, will recollect how everyone longed to see it covered with bright posters. Someone computed how much was lost by not letting this hoarding out. The sum was something enormous.

"THE BYSTANDER" by J. ASHBY-STERRY. "The Graphic." 10.12.92.

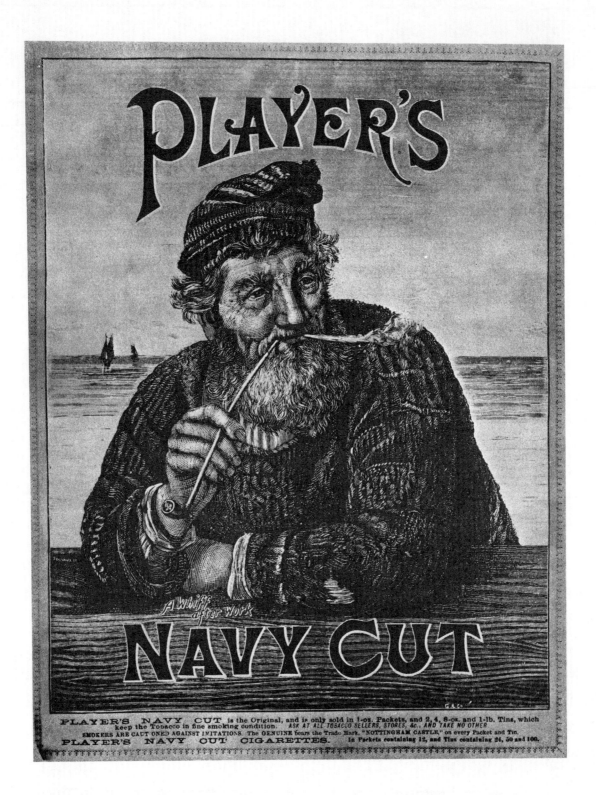

86

87

LONDON IN THE 90's

" A London of horse-trams with halfpenny fares, and of hansom-cabs ; of crystalline bells and spattering hoofs.   A London with winters of slush and fog of a richer sort than any known today, and summers of dust and calm ; the slush and dust being its heritage from the horse-traffic.   A London of solid homes, which regard the introduction of flat-life as something Not Quite Nice ; in fact, Fast . . . A London in which particular trades and callings still wore particular clothes . . . in which strong language, of a strength that would blanch these outspoken times, was used by certain men of all social classes . . . A London in which paper money, save in the five-ten-twenty series, was unthought of . . . A London which, as befitted a great metropolis, had nine evening papers . . . A London which was the centre of an Empire, and knew it . . .

Physically, it was dingy, and the general scene was by no means so fluent and coloured as it is today.   It had far fewer pleasures and public amenities ; most of the " gaiety " that one hears about took place within doors, and the public places caught only its aftermath in the form of reeling and uproarious young men."

From " LONDON IN MY TIME " *by Thomas Burke.*

" Love of town is a human passion which may not be suppressed by advocates of the Simple Life and the Return to Nature, even though they bedeck their propaganda with words of flame . . . For human life gravitates townwards . . . nothing, indeed, is more certain than the fact that, at the touch of humanity, the wilderness blossoms with the town . . . But during the Eighteen Nineties, as in one or two other periods of history, art threw a glamour over the town, and all the artificial things conjured up by that word . . . Poets no longer sought inspiration in solitude, they invoked the Muses in Fleet Street and the Strand . . .

In all this awakening interest in urban things, it is not surprising to learn that London inspired a renaissance of wonder . . . Not that the wonder of London was in any sense a new thing, even in literature. The capital city had inspired many a song, and many a purple patch of prose. But the men of the Nineties certainly added a new meaning to their worship of the great town."

From " THE EIGHTEEN-NINETIES " by *Holbrook Jackson.*

" This particular ' Literary movement ' of the nineties is an example of marionette-making, and the desire to classify and define has proved a snare to the industrious chronicler rather than a guide to his students. He bids us (' Observe, ladies and gentle-men ! ') notice the symptoms of revolt against Victorian conventions ; but under his efforts to make his figures dance, one arm jerks galvanically, the head turns, but the lips remain cataleptic. There is neither unity nor inherent life in his image, for, as a matter of fact, the revolt against Victorian conventions and reticences which is supposed to animate it had already taken place and had long ago been completely successful . . .
Before the dawn even of the nineties, the old idols had been quite toppled over, and the attempts to demonstrate that there was now marching out of the premises of the Bodley Head under the flying flag of *The Yellow Book* a band of April-eyed young brothers singing revolutionary ditties and bent on iconoclasm is disastrous to any clear conception of what was actually going on."

From " AS WE WERE " by *E. F. Benson.*

" As I see it, the function of the nineteenth century was to disengage the disinterested intelligence, to release it from the entanglements of party and sect—one might almost add of sex—and to set it operating over the whole range of human life and circumstance. In England we see this spirit issuing from, and often at war with, a society most stoutly tenacious of old ways and forms, and yet most deeply immersed in its new business of acquisition. In such warfare there is no victory, only victories, as something is won and held against ignorance or convention or prejudice or greed ; and in such victories our earlier and mid-Victorian time is rich. Not so the later. Much may be set to the account

90

of accident, the burden and excitement of Empire, the pressure of foreign armaments, the failure of individual genius, the distraction of common attention:. . . Compared with their fathers, the men of that time were ceasing to be a ruling or a reasoning stock ; the English mind sank towards that easily excited, easily satisfied, state of barbarism and childhood which press and politics for their own ends fostered, and on which in turn they fed . . ."

From " VICTORIAN ENGLAND " *by G. M. Young.*

" This I think can be said of the gay folk of the *fin-de-siècle*. If it be the prime object of life, as some distinguished authorities have maintained, to achieve happiness, these must be conceded quite an outstanding measure of success . . . For those at least who were on top of the world—and I think that this would apply below the top to a very considerable depth—it was a time of almost incredible plenty. The amount that people ate in those days had to be experienced to be believed . . .

As for the dinner parties, they were so popular a social function, they must, if they served no other purpose, have contributed in no small degree to the prosperity of the medical profession . . . Six solid main courses (not counting dessert) of heavy English cooking, not to speak of every sort of extra, were the least that any guest would have expected ; and an earnest devotion to the fare did at least tend to lighten the task of making heavier conversation . . . it seemed to me that most of the talk consisted of personal and local gossip on lines that soon became rigidly stereotyped . . .

Those were the sort of things that people took as seriously as it was in them to take anything . . . Not only religion, but even any pronounced form of irreligion, was too serious to thrive in this atmosphere. There were few open rebels against accepted dogma or convention, for rebellion requires a certain earnestness and concentration, and it is easier to drift with the stream. The façade of Victorian orthodoxy and respectability was maintained practically intact . . .

From " BEFORE THE LAMPS WENT OUT " *by Esme Wingfield-Stratford.*

THE EVENTS OF THE NINETIES IN LONDON	IN GREAT BRITAIN AND THE EMPIRE
1890 Freedom of City to H. M. Stanley, explorer. Strikes of postmen and police. New Corporation Art Gallery opened. Discovery of Roman remains at St. Martin-le-Grand. City and South London railway opened. " Baring " panic in City.	British protectorate over Zanzibar. General strikes in Australia.
1891 Bishopsgate Institute opened. London-Paris telephone inaugurated. Lord Mayor's appeal to Czar on behalf of Jews. Omnibus strike. State visit of Kaiser and Kaiserin.	Financial crisis and strikes in Australia.
1892 First sitting of London Chamber of Arbitration at Guildhall.	Gladstone Prime Minister.
1893 Royal Commission on Unification of London. Imperial Institute open to public. Guildhall banquet to King and Queen of Denmark, Prince and Princess of Wales and Czarevich. Wedding of Duke of York (later George V).	Gladstone's 2nd. Irish Home Rule Bill rejected. Matabele War. Natal given responsible government. New Zealand gives women the vote.
1894 Corporation refuses further evidence to Royal Commission. L.C.C.'s proposals : Lord Mayor, 19 Aldermen, 118 Councillors, adopted. Royal Commission recommends :— 1 Governing body with independent local bodies. Prince of Wales opens Tower Bridge. Equalization of Rates (London) Bill enacted. Anarchist Club in Windmill Street raided by the police.	Gladstone resigns—Lord Rosebery Prime Minister. Harcourt's " death duties " budget. British protectorate over Uganda. New Zealand Factory Inspection Act.
1895 City churches damaged by thunder and snow storms.	Lord Rosebery resigns—Lord Salisbury Prime Minister. Jameson Raid into Transvaal. British ultimatum to Transvaal.
1896 Southwark incorporated with London.	Victoria (Australia) Factory Wages Board Act. 1st outbreak of plague in India.
1897 £96,000 Fortifications (London) Bill given 1st reading. Dr. Nansen lectures to Royal Geographical Society.	Queen Victoria's Diamond Jubilee. Employers' Liability Act. Afridi and Mohmand rising on Indian frontier.
1898 Kitchener given freedom of City. Mansion House meeting to plan 1901 commemoration of death of King Albert.	Irish Local Government Act. Peace restored on Indian frontier.
1899 Metropolitan boroughs created by London Government Act.	O'Brien's United Irish League. Transvaal and Orange Free State declare war on Britain. Sieges of Ladysmith, Mafeking & Kimberley. Battles of Modder River, The Tugela and Magersfontein. Gold Rush to Klondyke. Anglo-Egyptian rule in Sudan.

EVENTS IN EUROPE	IN THE REST OF THE WORLD
1890 Death of William III of Holland. Wilhelmina succeeds to the throne. Fall of Bismarck in Germany. Fall of Tisza in Hungary. Heligoland ceded to Germany by Great Britain.	French protectorate over Madagascar. Anglo-French treaty delimits Lake Chad boundaries. 1st Japanese parliament.
1891 3 years famine starts in Russia. Anarchist outrages in Paris. German general insurance scheme completed.	Trans-Siberian railway begun. Close to Civil War in Chile.
1892 Wolte's financial reforms in Russia. French reconciliation with Papacy. French attack Dahomey and annex Ivory Coast.	Tewfik Pasha dies, succeeded by Abbas II; Egypt anti-British.
1893 Polish Socialist party formed.	Beginning of Civil War in Brazil.
1894 Death of Czar Alexander III. Succeeded by Nicholas II. President Carnot of France murdered. Trial of Captain Dreyfus begins in France. 10-year Russo-German Commercial treaty.	Turks massacre Armenians. Sino-Japanese War begins. Anglo-Japanese treaty of alliance. French at Timbuktu.
1895 Franco-Russian treaty of alliance. Ferdinand of Bulgaria recognised by Russia. Polish National League reorganised. Many mines and factories opened in S. Russia. Röntgen discovers X-Rays.	Queen of Korea murdered. More massacres in Armenia. France, Germany and Russia intervene between Japan and China. End of Sino-Japanese War. Secret Russo-Japanese treaty. End of Brazilian Civil War. Cuban rebellion.
1896	President Cleveland's Venezuela Message. French and British guarantee Siam. French annex Madagascar. Abyssinians defeat Italians at Adowa. Massacre of Armenians at Constantinople.
1897 Dreyfus agitation starts in France. Graeco-Turkish War.	Germany leases Kiaochow from China. Philippines revolt against Spain.
1898 Christians massacred. Britain, Russia, France and Italy occupy Crete. Czar calls Peace Conference. End of Franco-Italian Commercial " War " Near famine in Milan, riots and savage reprisals.	Destruction of the *Maine* in Havana Bay. U.S.—Spanish War. Santiago taken. Cuba separates. Treaty of Paris. U.S. takes Manila, annexes Philippines and Havana. Egyptians take Omdurman & Sudan. Marchand's expedition at Fashoda. Russia, Britain and France lease Chinese ports. Chinese Emperor abdicates in favour of Chinese Empress. Boxer movement begins in China.
1899 Death of Luis I of Portugal. Succeeded by Carlos I. Peace Conference at the Hague. Constitution of Finland abrogated by Czar. General Boulanger's plot defeated in France. End of Dreyfus affair in France. Macedonians demand independence.	Germany and U.S. divide Samoan Isles. Conclusion of Venezuela Boundary Arbitration.

CONTENTS

PHOTOGRAPHS

ACKNOWLEDGMENTS

Photographs on pages	10, 11, 12, 13, **14**, 15, 16, 18, 19, 20, 21, 22, 23, 24, 25, 26, 27, 28, 29, 30, 31, 33, 34, 35, 36, 37, 40, 41, 42, 43, 44, 45, 47, 49, 53, 54, 55, 56, 58, 59, 60, 61, 62, 63, 64, 66, 68, 69, 73, 76, 77, 78, 79, 82 and 83 by kind permission of W. G. Davies
Photograph on page	52 by kind permission of London Transport Executive
Photographs on pages	70 and 71 by kind permission of " The Autocar "
Photographs on page	38 by kind permission of the Ministry of Food
Photographs on pages	51, 57 and 80 by kind permission of Harris's Picture Agency
Advertisements on pages	85 and 87 by kind permission of Lever Bros. and Unilever Ltd.
Photographs on pages	48 and 50 by kind permission of the Council of Industrial Design
Advertisements on pages	84, 86 and 88 by kind permission of The Imperial Tobacco Co. Ltd.
Photographs on pages	9 and 75 by kind permission of The Times
Photograph on page	74 by courtesy of the Post Office

Extracts from Sir Max Beerbohm's " Works and More " by kind permission of Messrs. John Lane The Bodley Head.

Extracts from " Punch " by kind permission of the proprietors of " Punch."

Extracts from " City Press " by kind permission of the proprietors.

Extracts from " Murray's Magazine " and " London Past and Present " by H. B. Wheatley, by kind permission of Messrs. John Murray.

Extracts from " The National Review " by kind permission of the proprietors.

Extract from " Studio " by kind permission of the proprietors.

Extract from " Answers " by kind permission of Amalgamated Press Ltd.

Extract from " As We Were " by E. F. Benson, by kind permission of Mr. K. S. P. McDowall.

Extract from " The Eighteen-Nineties " by Holbrook Jackson, by kind permission of the Executors of the Holbrook Jackson Estate and the Society of Authors.

Extract from " Before the Lights Went Out " by E. Wingfield-Stratford, by kind permission of Messrs. Hodder and Stoughton, and Messrs. Christy and Moore, Ltd., Agents.

Extract from " Portrait of an Age " by G. M. Young, by kind permission of the Oxford University Press.

Extract from " London in My Time " by Thomas Burke, by kind permission of Messrs. Rich and Cowan, and Messrs. Farquharson, Agents.

It has been impossible to trace the present owners of the copyright of contributions to " All the Year Round " and " Pick-Me-Up."